CONF RMED
in the JOY of the SPIRIT

A Confirmation Journal for Teens
Inspired by
SAINTLY HEROES

TONY PICHLER *and* PAULA RIEDER

TWENTY-THIRD
PUBLICATIONS
twentythirdpublications.com

TWENTY-THIRD PUBLICATIONS
One Montauk Avenue, Suite 200
New London, CT 06320
(860) 437-3012 or (800) 321-0411
www.twentythirdpublications.com

Cover illustrations: Shutterstock

ISBN: 978-1-62785-344-6
Library of Congress Control Number: 2017958809
Printed in the U.S.A.

 A division of Bayard, Inc.

Contents

Contents

Introduction

Introduction

TWO PEOPLE ARE TRAVELING DOWN A ROAD, TALKING TO EACH OTHER ABOUT THE EVENTS THEY HAD JUST WITNESSED —the killing of their friend. This is not the latest fiction story that will serve as the basis for a Netflix series. This is the story of the disciples on the road to Emmaus that is found in the Gospel of Luke. It is this story that helps us to understand our own faith journey—especially during this time of preparation for the sacrament of confirmation.

These disciples of Jesus were trying to deal with the crucifixion of Jesus and make sense of it. Sometimes life is like that. We face some incredibly difficult challenges. But the two followers of Jesus did not face this challenge alone. They had each other. And we don't have to face our challenges alone either. We have each other too.

At other times, life gives us some really awesome experiences. And we do not always experience these alone either. We have parents. We have friends. We have companions on the journey.

In the same way, this journey to the sacrament of confirmation invites you to travel with others as well. You will have your parents, teachers, sponsor, and the entire parish community on the road with you.

On the road to Emmaus, the two disciples encountered the risen Christ. As you journey toward the sacrament of confirmation, you too will encounter the risen Christ in a special way.

It was in the breaking of the bread that the eyes of the two disciples were fully opened and they recognized Jesus in their midst. You have the opportunity to celebrate the Eucharist each week with the parish community and will continue to receive the strength and courage you need to continue on in the transformation of the world.

Finally, the two disciples were on fire when they recognized Jesus. In the same way, while the Holy Spirit has always been with you, guiding you on the journey of your life, in confirmation the Spirit will come to you in a special way. The prayer of the church community is that your heart will be burning with this faith and that you will be inspired to share your life and faith with those whom you encounter.

Classes, textbooks, retreats, service opportunities, conversations with a sponsor, catechists, and your parents are all available to help you on the journey. Lean on them! And know that they will guide you on the right path.

There are other disciples, other people of faith on the journey, who have come before you and can show you the path in a profound way. In this resource, you will encounter nineteen guides to help you. Each of them has a story to tell you, some wise words to live by, and an example to follow. Hopefully, you will be inspired by their stories and lives as you ask for the inspiration of the Holy Spirit.

Unlike many journeys you'll take, this is one trip that will last a lifetime. We have never fully arrived at life in the Spirit as we follow the example of Jesus. We explore this dimension of our faith very intensely and intentionally during this period of our life, but we know that we will always be deepening our faith in the risen Lord. This preparation for confirmation will be quite a journey! Enjoy the ride!

The Gifts of the Holy Spirit

AN OVERVIEW

WHAT IS THE BEST GIFT YOU HAVE EVER RECEIVED? Was it the latest game system? The newest version of a cell phone? Your first baseball glove? That outfit that you still love to wear? Or was it the gift of a sense of humor? Or the ability to learn languages easily? The ability to communicate in a public setting? No matter what the best gift was—object or attribute—this journey of confirmation promises an even better gift or, in this case, gifts!

The prophet Isaiah, foretelling the gifts of a future leader whom Christians identify with Jesus, names six gifts from Spirit of the Lord. Here are the words of Isaiah:

The spirit of the LORD shall rest upon him:
a spirit of wisdom and of understanding,
A spirit of counsel and of strength,
a spirit of knowledge and of fear of the LORD. **ISAIAH 11:2**

You are preparing to receive the Spirit of the Lord in a special way at confirmation. The Holy Spirit will enter your life in a special way and promises the best gifts you could ever receive:

**Wisdom • Understanding • Counsel • Fortitude
Knowledge • Piety • Wonder and Awe**

3

As you prepare for confirmation by attending classes, participating in service to others, making a retreat, journeying with a sponsor, and participating in your parish program, pay special attention to the promptings of the Holy Spirit in your life. The Spirit gives you life and love.

In the following pages you will be introduced to each of these gifts of the Holy Spirit. For each gift, you will also be introduced to a model of faith who can inspire you to live that gift in your life. Reflection questions will help you to ponder how you already have recognized the gifts of the Holy Spirit in your life. And you will be encouraged to take action using this particular gift in your life and preparation as a confirmation candidate.

Through the sacrament of confirmation, the gifts of the Holy Spirit are strengthened in you and help you to become a stronger witness to your faith in Jesus Christ. These are gifts that no friend or relative can wrap up and give to you following the celebration. Rather, these gifts will guide your faith, values, and actions for a lifetime! Come Holy Spirit, come!

CHAPTER ONE

The Gift of Wisdom

HENRI NOUWEN IS KNOWN AS THE GREAT
"WOUNDED HEALER." Born in 1932, Nouwen
became a priest, a professor at Yale and Notre
Dame, and a distinguished author. But the
one aspect of his life that captures the most
attention and gets chronicled in his countless books is his
search for peace in his own life and his ability to pass on
wisdom to others on the journey.

In 1974 Nouwen spent a year at a Trappist Abbey in search
of a new direction for his life. This time moved him to
believe that service as a missionary in Latin America was to
be his true calling. Yet, after spending time in Bolivia and
Peru, he returned to the United States, still in search of a
direction in his life.

The turning point came in 1986. He was invited to live in
a L'Arche community in Toronto, Canada, and serve as its
chaplain. L'Arche houses are residential communities for
adults who have cognitive and developmental disabilities.
Those who live in community provide daily care for the
residents. This was what Nouwen was ultimately called to,
living the rest of his life caring for Adam, a man who could
not talk or care for himself. It was in bathing, feeding, and
dressing Adam that Nouwen found the peace that he could

share with the world in his future writings.

Nouwen died of a heart attack in 1996. He left behind a library of classic works that continue to provide wisdom for all who read them.

The Gift of Wisdom

What exactly is wisdom? Unfortunately, many times we do not realize we have wisdom. It is not something we can order at a fast-food restaurant. It is not available on Amazon. Rather, wisdom is—pure and simple— something that we acquire through living life.

> ### The words of Henri Nouwen
>
> 66 Did I offer peace today? Did I bring a smile to someone's face? Did I say words of healing? Did I let go of my anger and resentment? Did I forgive? Did I love? These are the real questions. I must trust that the little bit of love that I sow now will bear many fruits, here in this world and the life to come."

Think of wisdom as a math equation. *Knowledge+lived experience=wisdom.* A fast-food restaurant employee can know everything there is to know about how to handle an angry customer. She may have read all of the books available on the topic. She may have attended a workshop or seminar entitled "How to Handle Angry Customers." In other words, she may have plenty of knowledge about handling angry customers. But until she adds the experience of actually *dealing* with angry customers—that person who gets a cold hamburger, or is missing french fries with his order—the employee will not have the wisdom of how best to handle angry customers. It is wisdom that is gained when she adds her knowledge to the actual experience of dealing with angry customers.

Grandparents, parents, coaches, teachers, an aunt, or an uncle are often the wisdom figures in our lives. They have gained valuable experience and knowledge through their years. This accumulation of experiences can often be very valuable when we enter into a situation that we have not yet encountered ourselves. If we are really open to listening, we can soak up the wisdom of these respected people in our life. Then, we can apply that wisdom to the situation we are in.

But here is the catch! As we go through life and experience various situations, *we* will be gaining wisdom. *We* might then become the wisdom figures sought out by a friend or younger brother or sister when they encounter a difficult situation. Then we can pray to the Holy Spirit for guidance as we impart this wisdom to them.

Maybe you will be one of those people who are termed "wise beyond their years." These people have a unique ability to be in tune with life and lived experiences to such a degree that they can incorporate the learning from these situations into future encounters with life. When a person is able to

The words of Henri Nouwen

" Each day holds a surprise. But only if we expect it can we see, hear, or feel it when it comes to us. Let's not be afraid to receive each day's surprise, whether it comes to us as sorrow or as joy. It will open a new place in our hearts, a place where we can welcome new friends and celebrate more fully our shared humanity."

do this, it is then that we say that she or he is "wise beyond their years"! May that person be *you!*

Here is a prayer, written by the theologian Reinhold Niebuhr, that asks for that wisdom we all seek:

God, grant me the serenity to accept the things I cannot change,
Courage to change the things I can,
And wisdom to know the difference.

Reflect

Wisdom is radiant and unfading, and she is easily discerned by those who love her, and is found by those who seek her. She hastens to make herself known to those who desire her. WISDOM 6:12–13

Who is a wisdom figure in your life? How does he or she show this wisdom to you?

_____

_____

_____

_____

_____

_____

_____

_____

In what areas of your life do you seek further wisdom?

_____

_____

_____

_____

_____

_____

Act

Imagine that you are seeking a wisdom figure in your life.
If you were to create a want ad for the local newspaper, what
knowledge, skills, and life experiences would you require
of such a person? Create your advertisement in the space
provided:

_____

_____

_____

_____

_____

_____

_____

_____

_____

CHAPTER TWO

The Gift of Understanding

MODEL OF FAITH ▸ *Pope Francis*

JORGE MARIO BERGOGLIO WAS BORN IN BUENOS AIRES, ARGENTINA, ON DECEMBER 17, 1936. After some early health difficulties and with his mother not necessarily agreeing to his vocational calling, he became a Jesuit priest in 1969. He quickly became a leader in the Jesuit religious order. In 1992 he became a bishop. In 1998 he became archbishop of Buenos Aires, his hometown. And on March 13, 2013, Archbishop Bergoglio became the 266th pope to lead the Roman Catholic Church, taking the name of Francis after his model of faith, St. Francis of Assisi. In the years following, Pope Francis has led this church of over a billion people with the gift of understanding, shepherding his flock with care, compassion, and humility.

The Gift of Understanding

A teen says to a parent: "You just don't understand me!!!"

A teacher says to the students: "You will need to understand this algebraic equation. It will be on the test."

One friend says to another: "You really understand where I'm coming from, don't you?"

A good definition of theology is "faith seeking

understanding" (St. Anselm). So what is understanding, and how is this a gift of the Holy Spirit? One way to look at understanding is to pull the word apart. To have understanding is to "stand under" some issue, challenge, or idea. You look at some aspect of your life or something that you are grappling with from a different perspective.

Did you ever get stuck with a problem? What helped you to eventually come to understand the situation? Perhaps it was that you took a step back and looked at the situation from a different perspective. You "stood under" (or around, or behind, or in front of) the problem. This truly is the gift of understanding!

It is this gift of the Holy Spirit that provides the ability to see life from different perspectives and so to understand our faith and the world a little better. But, as Pope Francis points out, this act of coming to understand is a discernment process. It does not come easily. And as he says, we must leave room for doubt in our life. We will probably never fully understand everything in our life because of our human limitations. But the journey of life entails gaining a bit more understanding each and every day. As the saying goes: life is a journey—enjoy the ride!

Holy Spirit, please give me the gift of understanding!

> **The words of Pope Francis**
>
> " My choices, including those related to the day-to-day aspects of life, like the use of a modest car, are related to a spiritual discernment that responds to a need that arises from looking at things, at people, and from reading the signs of the times. Discernment in the Lord guides me in my way of governing."

Reflect

[The lawyer] answered, "You shall love the Lord your God with all your heart, and with all your soul, and with all your strength, and with all your mind; and your neighbor as yourself." And [Jesus] said to him, "You have given the right answer; do this, and you will live."

LUKE 10:27–28

Reflect on your understanding of God's love in your life. How do you experience that love? How is God calling you to love others?

_____

_____

_____

_____

_____

Many times, different emotions arise as we try to seek understanding in the various situations of our life. What emotion do you need help with as you seek the gift of understanding from the Holy Spirit?

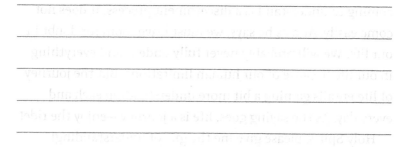

Act

Below are three quotes, all examples of how we can come to understand our life and world through our everyday experiences:

"It hurts me when I see a priest or nun with the latest modern car. You can't do this. A car is necessary to do a lot of work, but please, choose a more humble one. If you like the fancy one, just think about how many children are dying of hunger in the world." **POPE FRANCIS**

"Today I went to a nursing home, and I played Wii with the residents. I was nervous because I was not sure what to say or do when I got there. As we started to play and I began to see the personalities of each resident come to life, I saw how the effects of age, and how it hindered their physical abilities, were present in the lives of many residents. They were having fun even though I had to help some people hold on to the controllers.

"I began to understand that it was not the game that was important but the relationship that was forming through my insecurities and their vulnerability. I learned a lot that day, and realize that, even though we are different, we have much in common." **SHANE**

"At the lunch table my friends and I were talking about the upcoming weekend. Kathy, who is one of my friends, was talking about having another drinking party at her house. Her parents know about the parties and they even supply the beer. Kathy and I are both on the basketball team, and I just don't feel right about going. Not only would I be breaking the law but also breaking the athletic code that I signed in the beginning of the school year.

I feel the peer pressure of going to the party, but I also recognize the feelings going on inside of me.

"As I discern this situation I look at why I am afraid to say no to my friend Kathy. I see my own insecurities and false hope that I put into this relationship and find that these insecurities and false hopes are based on my own fears. I see that the security I look for does not come from others but comes from the courage it takes to live an authentic life." **SAMANTHA**

The gift of understanding calls us to act in truth—a truth found in a spiritual understanding that brings the light of Christ to the human needs and desires that we encounter in our lives.

If you found yourself in one or more of the scenarios above, what actions could you take in order to understand the situation from a different perspective?

_____

_____

_____

_____

_____

_____

_____

_____

CHAPTER THREE

The Gift of Counsel

MODEL OF FAITH ▶ *St. Thomas More*

THOMAS MORE WAS A LAWYER, JUDGE, AND SCHOLAR WHO BECAME A MARTYR FOR HIS FAITH AT THE BEGINNING OF THE REFORMATION IN THE EARLY 1500S. King Henry VIII of England named Thomas to the post of lord chancellor. In doing this, the king promoted Thomas to the highest rank possible for someone who was not born into royalty. He was a dedicated and wise man who served his country and his king with wisdom and counsel.

But a problem arose. King Henry wanted to divorce his wife, Catherine of Aragon, and marry Anne Boleyn. This practice was against the normal practice of the Catholic Church. Henry appealed his case to the pope, but the pope ruled that Henry could not make this move. King Henry did so anyway and renounced the ruling by the pope. Taking it a step further, the king forced everyone to sign an oath of allegiance to him, acknowledging him to be supreme head of both church and state in England. Thomas More refused to sign this oath. Thomas More was arrested and imprisoned and eventually beheaded on July 6, 1535. His feast day as a martyr for the faith is June 22.

The Gift of Counsel

Do you ever wonder if you are doing the right thing when faced with a difficult choice or decision in life? "What college should I attend? What career should I pursue? Should I get married? Stay single? Or accept the call to a religious vocation?" All are difficult decisions to make in our lives. So how do we decide? What is the right option to choose? Do we ever know? So many questions and so little time!

> ### The words of St. Thomas More
> " I die the king's faithful servant, but God's first."

The gift of counsel is the ability to decide right from wrong and to help others come to that same understanding. During difficult times of decision, guided by the Holy Spirit, here are some things we can do to put the gift of counsel to use:

❶ Bringing our decision-making process to prayer is always the best place to start! Ask the Holy Spirit for guidance, wisdom, and peace in the process that you are going to undertake.

❷ List all of your options for the decision you need to make. It is never a bad idea to take out a sheet of paper, put a line down the middle of the sheet, and on one side place the heading "Pros" and on the other "Cons." Place all of the good things that might result from the decision on the "Pro" side. Place all of the potentially negative aspects of the decision on the "Con" side. It rarely is as simple as adding up the columns to see which one gets the most comments, thus making your decision for you. But by seeing the potential results, you might get a good indication of which direction you should go.

Ask the counsel of some wisdom figures in your life. Parents, grandparents, sponsors, neighbors, teachers, coaches, and trusted friends are all people who know you, value the decisions that you make in your life, and can probably give you some valuable input.

 Follow your gut. What do you feel inside? What, if anything, is making you uneasy about this decision? Do you have this "deep down" feeling that seems to indicate which direction you should turn? Usually that is a good sign that you should make the decision in that direction.

Remember, even though you use some or all of the steps in this process, it is sometimes only in hindsight that we truly know if we made the correct decision or not. It might

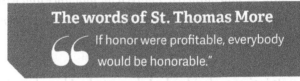
The words of St. Thomas More

" If honor were profitable, everybody would be honorable."

be months or even years until we really know if we decided correctly. But what is the alternative? Decision paralysis! In other words, not making any decision at all. So don't get paralyzed by difficult decisions. Ask for the gift of counsel, and the presence of the Holy Spirit in your life, and chances are you will have a lifetime of going down the right path— just like St. Thomas More!

Reflect

Read these two statements, by Erin and by Joel.

"Today is the day I need to decide what colleges I am going to be visiting. Mom and Dad, along with relatives, have been asking me the question, 'What do you want to spend your life doing?' Wow, I was overwhelmed. So I asked my uncle to help me. He and I always had fun together. I always felt that he understood me and wanted the best for me. His help was great. He asked me questions, helped me research, and always wanted to counsel me. He and I made a list of careers and opportunities that I thought I would enjoy and be good at. We researched the colleges that would best help me reach my goal, and then my uncle left me to reflect and decide upon all the data we had gathered. I prayed for guidance and wisdom as I looked within myself to find the answers that brought the most peace and comfort in making my decision." ERIN

"It is time to decide who I choose to be. I have been trying to fit into a group of kids for two years, and for two years I have felt a struggle within myself. I never quite feel as though I fit in with those kids I hang around with. I have noticed in their conversations that they do things together and rarely ask me to join in. And when we are together, in my gut I've felt that the choices I have to make have not felt like choices I would choose. Who am I, what do I believe, and who in my life supports and makes me a better person?

"As I discern who and what is a true friend I begin listing those people who make me feel accepted and wanted. These friends help counsel, guide, and support me as I pray to the Holy Spirit for the wisdom to make decisions that bring me peace in my everyday life."
JOEL

Have you ever needed to make a decision like Erin or Joel? What was involved in the decision?

_____

_____

_____

How was your decision similar? How was your decision different from theirs?

_____

_____

_____

Why is it difficult to make certain choices in our life?

_____

_____

Act

The gift of counsel calls us to search our heart, mind, and soul as we make life choices. What is a choice that you need to make in your life right now? Using the formula above, map out your direction for this decision:

_____

_____

_____

Write a short prayer of guidance to the Holy Spirit:

_____

_____

_____

_____

List your options:

_____

_____

_____

Ask a trusted wisdom figure about your options. What is their response?

_____

_____

_____

Does your choice bring you a sense of peace, or are you uneasy with your decision? Describe your feelings if you are able:

_____

_____

_____

_____

_____

CHAPTER FOUR

The Gift of Fortitude

MODEL OF FAITH — *Cesar Chavez*

CESAR CHAVEZ WAS A MEXICAN AMERICAN WHO WAS BORN IN 1927 IN THE SOUTHWESTERN PART OF THE UNITED STATES. His family lost their farm in the Great Depression and they were forced to become migrant workers, moving up and down the West Coast, working the land for a meager wage. As Cesar married and became the father of several children, he wanted to gain a better life for his family. Inspired by a priest and other social activists, Cesar became a community organizer, forming other migrant workers into a union—later to become the United Farm Workers Union. The apex of the union occurred in the later 1960s as Cesar called for a boycott of table grapes. A national movement was born!

Cesar also showed incredible fortitude as he underwent food fasts to draw attention to the cause of the migrant worker. Dorothy Day and Robert Kennedy were among the notable people who supported him and his cause. Cesar died on April 23, 1993, after a long struggle for justice. Through his fortitude in the face of hardship, he had raised the standard of living for the migrant workers in this country.

The Gift of Fortitude

The lion in the *Wizard of Oz* journeys down the yellow brick road with Dorothy, the scarecrow, and the tin man looking for one thing that was missing in his life: courage. But along the way he fights off flying monkeys, battles a wicked witch, and stares down the Wizard of Oz himself. The courage he was looking for on the long journey to Oz was something that already existed inside of himself. He just needed to recognize it and be affirmed by others.

What is the gift of fortitude? It is the strength necessary to face adversity with courage. Have you been in situations where you needed fortitude? Perhaps you were on the basketball court, down by one point with three seconds to go. Maybe you were a track runner trying to achieve that personal record in the race. Or perhaps you were performing in the school play and needed to recite numerous lines from memory. All of these examples take fortitude.

In life, there are moments when fortitude is necessary. We will experience pressure to use alcohol or other drugs, join a gang, or engage in sexual activities. As we face each one, the Spirit gives us the gift of fortitude to endure and thrive in the difficult times of our lives. Like the lion in the Wizard of Oz, we will hopefully realize that we have had the inner

The words of Cesar Chavez

> It is possible to become discouraged about the injustice we see everywhere. But God did not promise us that the world would be humane and just. He gives us the gift of life and allows us to choose the way we will use our limited time on earth. It is an awesome opportunity. "

fortitude that we needed all along. We just need to recognize it and affirm it—in ourselves and others!

Reflect

I want to do something meaningful in life, but what? I look with fortitude to see within myself the truth so that I may find the strength to act on the gifts that I possess.

Who are the people in your life who help guide you in finding your fortitude?

_____

_____

_____

_____

_____

_____

What strengths and gifts can you find within yourself to act on your desires?

_____

_____

_____

_____

_____

_____

Act

Consider a random act of kindness. You know—the kind of act that is unexpected but that will do something good for someone else. Think about your strengths and talents. What random act can you do that will take a little fortitude on your part? List it here, and then get to work!

_____

_____

_____

_____

_____

_____

_____

_____

_____

_____

_____

_____

_____

CHAPTER FIVE

The Gift of Knowledge

MODEL OF FAITH ▸ *St. Thomas Aquinas*

St. Thomas Aquinas is arguably one of the most knowledgeable persons in church history. But it was not always so. Thomas was born in 1225 in southern Italy to a wealthy family. The youngest of four boys, he was sent by his parents to a Benedictine monastery where they thought he would be raised in the Benedictine way of life but also set up the family with additional wealth and honor. But Thomas wanted nothing of this plan! He wished to become a Dominican friar. After a struggle, his family finally gave in, and Thomas entered the Order of Preachers.

Thomas studied at Cologne but was so intimidated by the abilities of the other students that he remained silent during classes. His classmates translated this silence into a belief that Thomas was actually stupid. On the contrary, Thomas was a brilliant student. He went on to earn a doctorate at the University of Paris, where he taught for the better part of his career.

Thomas' genius was his ability to incorporate philosophy, most notably that of Aristotle, into his theological writings. This was not always favorably regarded by the religious leaders of his time. His most important work, the *Summa Theologiae*, was a classic example of his theological depth.

But while he never finished the work, he became the most influential theologian for hundreds of years—right into the twentieth century—and his work was used to train future priests in seminaries all over the world.

Thomas died at the age of 49 in 1274. He is a doctor of the church, which means that he is a person who is held up as a great teacher.

The Gift of Knowledge

The life of St. Thomas Aquinas illustrates the importance of seeking knowledge throughout one's lifetime. His life shows that it is not so important *how* we gain knowledge; but rather, *that* we seek new ways to learn.

Knowledge is gained in two distinct ways: through academic learning and through the learning that occurs through lived experience. Some would call this the "school of hard knocks." Whether it is through experiential learning or gaining knowledge from books and classes, the gift of knowledge is acquired in four ways:

> **The words of St. Thomas Aquinas**
>
> 66 To one who has faith, no explanation is necessary. To one without faith, no explanation is possible."

1 **Head:** There are certain bits of knowledge that we gain through reading, attending a class, or watching a video. This knowledge is more logic based and is centered more in our head. While this information is vitally important, if you only learned the facts about your faith, you most likely would not live as a Christian because the other dimensions of your being would not be affected.

2   *Heart:* Certain knowledge affects our heart. Some things we learn from our very being by sinking deep into us and causing us to *be* different people. This knowledge affects our feelings and beliefs. Again, if we only learn through our heart, we may not gain wider perspective of our faith and how to enact our beliefs.

3   *Hands:* Some knowledge causes us to act on our faith. This is knowledge that goes beyond our head and our hearts and stirs us to use our hands to reach out to others; especially those in need or living on the margins. This knowledge helps us to become closer to the reality of others' lived experience.

4   *Feet:* Lastly, some knowledge causes us to take a stand for our convictions and beliefs. We can learn the facts of our faith. We can be touched by how the faith changes us. And we can enact our faith by reaching out. But sometimes it is the strong voice that needs to be heard and unmask the reality that some people face. This is when our faith is truly lived!

The words of St. Thomas Aquinas

❝ Faith has to do with things that are not seen, and hope with things that are not at hand."

If St. Thomas Aquinas were alive today he would probably say that all four dimensions of seeking knowledge are important. They are best when used together—as a unified whole. But Thomas would also include prayer and contemplation as part of how we gain our knowledge of God and others. He even told his companion, Fr. Reginald, that he learned more from prayer and contemplation than he did from books and experiences. If we take St. Thomas Aquinas seriously as a model of the gift of knowledge, then we will ask the Holy Spirit to touch our whole being, including our prayer and contemplation, as we learn more about God.

Reflect

Using the results from the tool above, in what ways do you learn best?

In what ways do you struggle to learn?

_____

_____

_____

_____

_____

_____

_____

Act

There is the old saying that you learn best by teaching. Think of something that you can teach another person about living his or her faith. Describe it here:

_____

_____

_____

_____

_____

_____

_____

_____

Now decide what learning style you could use from the list above. What strategies will you use to teach the person what you want to get across to him/her? List them here:

_____

_____

_____

_____

_____

_____

_____

Go, ahead! Start teaching!

CHAPTER SIX

The Gift of Piety

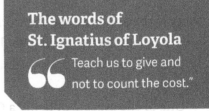

MODEL OF FAITH

St. Ignatius of Loyola

SOMETIMES LIFE PRESENTS TWISTS AND TURNS THAT ARE NOT NECESSARILY EXPECTED. Such was the life of Ignatius of Loyola! Íñigo López de Loyola was born in Spain in 1491. He was born into a noble family and was trained to be of service to the Spanish king. But in a battle against the French, young Ignatius was injured badly. While his injuries were healing, he read the lives of the saints. In doing so he decided to change his life, turn to God, and dedicate himself to serving the glory of God.

While on a pilgrimage, Ignatius laid down his sword and became a "soldier of Christ." He then traveled to the Holy Land and while there answered a call to the priesthood. He set off for Paris and studied at the University of Paris. It was there that Ignatius convinced a group of six men to join him in a new religious community. Thus was born the Society of Jesus, known as the Jesuits.

The words of St. Ignatius of Loyola

❝ Teach us to give and not to count the cost."

Ignatius was not only known for founding a religious community, he was also respected for his spiritual prayer practices that came through in his famous work, the *Spiritual*

Exercises. In this classic work, Ignatius proposed a method of examining one's faith life that was to be done using the format of a thirty-day retreat. Ignatian spirituality has become one of the hallmarks of Christian spirituality. Ignatius died in 1556. His order had increased from six to one thousand men by the time of his death.

The Gift of Piety

St. Patrick, the great saint of Ireland, had a prayer that we call St. Patrick's Breastplate. His words, in part, were these:

> *Christ with me, Christ before me,*
> *Christ behind me,*
> *Christ in me, Christ beneath me,*
> *Christ above me,*
> *Christ on my right, Christ on my left,*
> *Christ when I lie down, Christ when I sit,*
> *Christ when I stand,*

Piety is the ability to see the world through the eyes of faith and to recognize God in all people and all created things. Both Saint Patrick and Saint Ignatius Loyola serve as models of piety.

One of the aspects of being a Catholic Christian is seeing the world through sacramental eyes. What does this mean? A sacrament is anything that God uses to make God present to us. Our church has seven formal sacraments. Baptism, confirmation, Eucharist, reconciliation, marriage, holy orders, and anointing of the sick are all ways that God is present to us in a special way.

But God can also be present to us in our family or friends, the work that we do, the nature that we enjoy, or the sports or other activities in which we participate. All have the ability to show us another aspect or side of God and present an opportunity for God to relate to us.

In his famous method of prayer, the *Examen,* St. Ignatius of Loyola provides us with a tool to reflect on our day and recall the ways that God has been present to us each day. How does it work? Here are the steps of the *Examen* that St. Ignatius proposes:

1. Become aware of God's presence; Look back on your day and all that happened. Our lives are so busy and can become a blur. But recall as much as you can about your day.

2. Review the day with gratitude: When were the times you felt the presence of God in the people you met or the activities in which you were engaged?

3. Pay attention to your emotions: When were the times that you were most filled with joy? or anxiety? or anger? or confidence? Bring to mind these emotions that God has gifted you with.

4. Choose one aspect of your day and pray with it: Take one event, person, or emotion from your day and use that to pray spontaneously. Have a conversation with God about that. No need for memorized prayers here. Just sit with God for a while.

5. Look forward to the next day. As you look ahead to tomorrow, what is it that you would like to ask God? Is there an important event going on at school? Is there a person you need to have a conversation with that causes you anxiety? Bring that to prayer. Ask for God's presence in a special way as you head into the coming day.

Gerard Manley Hopkins was a Jesuit priest and poet who lived in the mid 1800s. He described the world as "charged with the grandeur of God." Seeing the world this way is a gift that the Holy Spirit gives to us as we receive piety.

The words of St. Ignatius of Loyola

66 For those who love, nothing is too difficult, especially when it is done for the love of our Lord Jesus Christ."

Reflect

When you are reflecting on your day or moment of time, remember that the steps of the *Examen* can be changed around. Your feelings will sometimes determine what steps need to be taken first in order for you to move forward.

Act

Journal the wisdom and truth you find when you learn to see the beauty and the chains that bind you and others. Use the above steps in growing through a situation that you are experiencing now. *"Love one another as I have loved you."*

_____

_____

_____

_____

_____

_____

_____

_____

_____

_____

CHAPTER SEVEN

The Gift of Wonder and Awe

MODEL OF FAITH

Pierre Teilhard de Chardin

PIERRE TEILHARD DE CHARDIN WAS GIFTED WITH WONDER AND AWE IN A NUMBER OF WAYS. As a scientist, priest, and theologian, Teilhard drew together insights and inspiration from the fields of theology, science, and spirituality. But his life was filled with challenges—which makes his sense of wonder and awe even more special!

Teilhard was born on May 1, 1881. He entered the Society of Jesus (Jesuits) at the age of eighteen. As a scientist, he was part of the team in the 1920s that discovered the remains of the Peking Man, which were the oldest remains of any human beings discovered up to that time.

Teilhard had a view of evolution that was unusual for the early twentieth century. He believed that humans and God form a sort of co-creation in which the world was still evolving and working out its ultimate destiny—union with God.

But it was because of these unique views that Teilhard was forbidden by his religious superiors to teach or publish any religious books. His tremendous faith kept him writing and working. Many of his books were published after his death.

Teilhard died on Easter Sunday, 1955. To him, the world was certainly charged with the beauty of God. As a man ahead of his time, he used this wonder and awe to bring other believers to faith in God.

The Gift of Wonder and Awe

One way to consider the gift of wonder and awe is to ponder the history of the creation of our world. That is something that Pierre Teilhard de Chardin did in his work as a scientist and man of faith. Think of the history of our world as if it were all created in a single day. What would that look like? Consider that any form of life did not show up until 3:00 in the morning. Seaweed (yes seaweed!) did not appear until 8:28 p.m. Land plants were not created until 9:52 p.m. Dinosaurs appeared at 10:56 p.m. Mammals came along at 11:39 p.m. And then,

> ### The words of Pierre Teilhard de Chardin
>
> " Someday, after mastering the winds, the waves, the tides and gravity, we shall harness for God the energies of love, and then, for a second time in the history of the world, man will have discovered fire. "

finally, humans were created at 11:58:43. That is 17 seconds before midnight. Yes, humans are extremely important in God's creative plan, but we did not come around until very late in the game. That means that all of the other works of God are important as well—and predate us by a long shot!

The gift of wonder and awe helps us keep our place in creation in perspective. It helps us to see all of God's creation, from the smallest insect to the magnificent Grand Canyon, as breathtaking and beautiful.

How we care for God's creation goes a long way toward affirming a sense of wonder and awe in us. More than just recycling our soda cans, or putting trash in its proper place, how we take care of the earth proves whether we are good stewards of the earth or not. Stewards are not owners. They are merely caretakers of something that is owned by someone else. In this case the owner of the world is God. We are merely called to be stewards of it—to take care of it to the best of our ability.

> **The words of**
> **Pierre Teilhard de Chardin**
>
> 66 The world is round so that friendship may encircle it."

Sometimes we hear people describing the world as being awful. This is awful and that is awful. But seeing the world through sacramental eyes—seeing the beauty of God in all of creation—can change that attitude. So, instead of being awful, the world becomes AWE FULL!

So, pray for the gift of wonder and awe from the Holy Spirit. And then roll up your sleeves and get to work in caring for this gift of the world that God has given to us!

Reflect

Do you remember experiencing your first fireworks or seeing your first Christmas light show or catching your first fish? Write down one of your most memorable moments and the way it made you feel inside.

_____

_____

_____

_____

Act

As you continue to grow in the depths of awe and wonder, learn to experience the joys of others. Take time out of your day to listen to someone else share about a period of time in their life. Try to make a connection with the feelings that they are sharing. Write down what you noticed when you lovingly listened to another person. Where did you see God? Next, take time out of your day to enjoy nature or time to reflect on life. Write down your thoughts and express where you see God.

_____

_____

_____

_____

The Fruits
of the Holy Spirit
AN OVERVIEW

HAVE YOU EVER PICKED AN APPLE OR ORANGE FROM A TREE?
If not, imagine doing so. What does the fruit look like?
Is it plump and juicy? Is the fruit perfect or does it have
imperfections or flaws? Do you think the tree is "hurt" by
you picking this fruit?

St. Paul's Letter to the Galatians in the first century
provides a spiritual description of what fruits are available
to you as a Christian living a life as a disciple or follower of
Jesus. Here are Paul's words:

> *"The fruit of the Spirit is love, joy, peace, patience, kindness,*
> *generosity, faithfulness, gentleness, and self-control."*
> **GALATIANS 5:22–23**

Let's go back to our apples and oranges. How do we know a
bad apple or orange tree from a good one? By its fruit! Does
the fruit look good? Does it taste good? Does it have to be
perfect to be good? Of course not! And is the tree damaged
by you picking the fruit from its branches? That is what
makes a tree what it is—it produces fruit and gives it away.

So let us apply the tree analogy to you. How do you know
that you are following Jesus and being the disciple that he
wants you to be as a person in relationship to him? Again, by

your fruit! How are you living? What actions do you take on a daily basis to truly live as his follower?

In the sacrament of confirmation, the gifts of the Holy Spirit strengthen us to live as disciples of Jesus. In doing so, they produce in us good fruit. The fruits of the Holy Spirit are:

**Charity (Love) • Joy • Peace • Patience
Kindness • Goodness • Generosity
Gentleness • Faithfulness • Modesty
Self-Control • Chastity**

Just as you experienced with the gifts of the Holy Spirit, in the following pages each fruit will be explained, a model of our faith who especially shows each fruit will be provided, and several journal reflection questions and some suggested action ideas will be presented.

As you work through these pages, challenge yourself to reflect upon the type of fruit you are producing already. Where do you most need the help of the Holy Spirit in producing even more plentiful and quality fruit? And how generous are you in giving away the fruits with which God has blessed you? And just like those apple and orange trees, you do not need to be perfect, and your fruits need not be either. Jesus just wants you to do your best and keep the growing process going!

CHAPTER EIGHT

The Fruit of Charity

MODEL OF FAITH → *St. Teresa of Calcutta*

IF YOU LOOK UP *CHARITY* IN A DICTIONARY, YOU JUST MIGHT SEE A PICTURE OF ST. TERESA OF CALCUTTA IN THE MARGIN. But she was not always known for her charity. Born in Albania, she answered the call to be a Sister of Loreto and was stationed in India where she served as a school teacher for twenty years. Then she received what she termed "a call within a call." While traveling by train in the Himalayas in 1946, she felt God "wanted me to be poor with the poor, and love him in the distressing disguise of the poorest of the poor." So she went to Calcutta, India, and formed a community of sisters known as the Missionaries of Charity. She herself became known as Mother Teresa.

She served the poorest of the poor in the slums of Calcutta. She helped these "least of our brothers and sisters" who lived like "animals in the gutters" to "die like angels." Her work earned her a Nobel Peace Prize. It also gained her the respect of people around the world. She was known for her tremendous charity and love. Little by little, she formed ministry centers around the world with thousands of sisters following her example.

Yet her work was not without a dark side. Her journals, published after her death in 1997, showed a deeply religious woman who questioned the presence of God in her life. It was a struggle that would last a lifetime.

Mother Teresa was beatified in 2003 and became St. Teresa of Calcutta in 2016.

The Fruit of Charity

There is a church hymn entitled "They'll Know We are Christians By Our Love." The words form the basis of this fruit of the Holy Spirit. How will someone know that you are a Christian? How did Jesus instruct his disciples to follow him? By loving one another. At the core of our Christian faith lies this fruit—love.

It is said that there are fifty Eskimo words for snow. Snow that is heavy and can easily be created into a snowball or a snowman gets one word. Light, fluffy snow gets assigned a different word. Likewise, there is more than one word for love, or at least there was in the original Greek language in which the New Testament was written. Three words for love in Greek are *eros*, *philio*, and *agape*. Sound complicated? Well, not really!

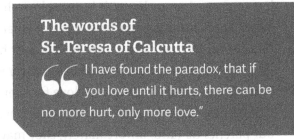

The words of St. Teresa of Calcutta

" I have found the paradox, that if you love until it hurts, there can be no more hurt, only more love."

Eros love is the love that a man might feel for a woman or vice versa. This is a passionate love in which two people are physically attracted to each other. It is the love that you see on TV or in the movies. It might be the love that is portrayed on billboards or in magazine ads. Or, it might be the love that you feel welling up inside you as you sit next to that boy or girl in math class! Eros love is the love of passion. But it can be fleeting. It can come and go as our emotions change. Eros love is not necessarily a deep love or a lasting love.

Philio love is quite literally "brotherly" (or "sisterly") love. There is a reason that Philadelphia is named as such. It is the "City of Brotherly Love" and it has *philio* at it root. When we love a brother or sister, or a teammate or friend, we are loving them with *philio* love. It is different from *eros* love in that it is not built on passion. Rather, *philio* love is enduring—many times lasting a lifetime. Communities are built on *philio* love, communities such as families, churches, sports teams and friendship groups.

Then there is *agape* love. This is the unconditional love of one for another. God has *agape* love for us. God loves us for who we are—warts and all! And God, through Jesus, calls us to have *agape* love for one another. If someone betrays us, lies to us, or does us harm, it is *agape* love that forgives them. Why? Because with *agape* love, it is not what someone does to us or for us that causes us to love him or her. Rather, we love the person for who he or she is, not for what they do. Parents are called to have *agape* love for their children, and children for their parents. We might not always like what our parents do (and, unfortunately, they may not always be pleased with us either!) But, with *agape* love we still love our parents, and they love us. This unconditional love is a gift from the heart. In this way, it brings us to the richest meaning of love. To be a person of charity means to be a person of great love.

The Holy Spirit gives us an opportunity to love each other with *agape* love. It is by this fruit that the words of St. Paul to the people of Corinth ring true—even to today: "Love is patient, love is kind. It is not jealous, [love] is not pompous, it is not inflated, it is not rude, it does not seek its own interests, it is not quick-tempered, it does not brood over injury, it does not rejoice over wrongdoing but rejoices with the truth. It bears all things, believes all things, hopes all things, endures all things. Love never fails" (1 Corinthians 13:4–8).

Reflect

Two years ago, Kelly wanted to go out with her friends and her parents would not let her go. She was so angry that she did not speak to them for weeks. It was later that she realized that her parents were right and loved her unconditionally.

Who has provided you with unconditional love?

_____

_____

_____

_____

How did you know that this love was unconditional?

_____

_____

_____

_____

What circumstances were involved that showed you this type of love?

_____

_____

_____

Act

What opportunity can you create for another person that allows them to experience unconditional love?

What steps do you need to take in order to enact this plan?

Step One: _____

Step Two: _____

Step Three: _____

Once you have completed your action, how does it feel to show unconditional love to another person?

_____

_____

_____

CHAPTER NINE

The Fruit of Joy

MODEL OF FAITH ▶ *Sr. Thea Bowman*

SISTER THEA BOWMAN WAS A WOMAN OF GREAT JOY! Born in Mississippi in 1937, Thea (then known as Bertha) went to a Catholic school and converted to Catholicism when she was nine years old. At sixteen, Thea felt called to the religious life and became a Franciscan Sister of Perpetual Adoration, based in La Crosse, Wisconsin.

At first, Thea did not have much that should have caused her joy. She was the only black sister in an all-white community. But Thea refused to blend in. She desired to live fully her African American culture *and* her Catholicism. She wanted to bring her whole person as an African American woman to her teaching and preaching.

After earning a doctorate degree, Sr. Thea returned to Mississippi and Louisiana to minister to African Americans in the south. She was instrumental in founding the Institute of Black Catholic Studies at Xavier University in New Orleans.

In 1984 Sr. Thea was diagnosed with cancer. She continued to speak to groups around the country, including the U.S. Catholic bishops, even when in a wheelchair as her illness progressed.

Sr. Thea Bowman died in 1990. She was 53 years old.

The Fruit of Joy

The fruit of joy comes from God. Joy is the conviction that
God lies at the core of all that we are and all that we do.
Joy gives us serenity in knowing that it is God who gives us
strength, courage, and peace to forge ahead—even when
times get tough. In the example of a model of faith above,
Sr. Thea Bowman lived with great joy. She was grounded in a
love for God and a core conviction that God loved her. It was
this great joy that oozed out of her every time she spoke to
a group or met any individual. Sr. Thea certainly had some
rough days, especially as she battled cancer. But her joy was
always evident.

Was Sr. Thea always happy? Probably not! There were
challenges in her life, especially as a black sister in a white
community.
But joy is not
happiness and
happiness is not
joy. Happiness

> ### The words of Sr. Thea Bowman
> " Remember who you are and whose
> you are."

can be more fleeting than joy, whereas joy is a constant in
life. Pope Francis reminds us: "If we live the faith in our daily
life, then our work too becomes a chance to spread the joy of
being a Christian."

God calls us, in a relationship with God, to be joyful
always. St. Paul, in his letter to the people of Philippi, said:
"Rejoice in the Lord always. I shall say it again: rejoice!"
(Philippians 4:4). It is when our lives are grounded in
something lasting, in a relationship with God as shown in
our love and concern for those around us, that we will have
great joy.

Reflect

What person in your life exudes joy? How do you experience this joy?

_____

_____

_____

_____

_____

If a friend needs a concrete example of this difference between joy and happiness, what actions can you use to help him or her to understand?

_____

_____

_____

_____

_____

Act

Go to a local nursing home and sit with an elderly person. Allow them to tell you what brought them joy in their life. Take note! Their joy may become yours!

CHAPTER TEN

The Fruit of Peace

St. Teresa Benedicta of the Cross

EDITH STEIN WAS BORN ON OCTOBER 12, 1891, INTO A JEWISH FAMILY. It happened to be Yom Kippur, the Jewish Day of Atonement. Later, Edith would see this as a sign, or foreshadowing, of her future fate.

Edith pursued a degree in philosophy and proved to be a brilliant student. Following the death and destruction of World War I, Edith became very much interested in religion. One night in 1921, Edith went to bed reading St. Teresa of Ávila's autobiography. It changed her life. The life of this holy, sixteenth-century Carmelite nun had a profound effect on the young Edith. By the time the sun rose, Edith had decided to convert to Catholicism.

The conversion to Catholicism was very difficult on Edith's mother. To appease her mother, Edith went to Mass but also attended services at the Jewish synagogue. She felt that Christianity and Judaism went hand in hand.

The Nazi Party in Germany began to persecute Jews, causing Edith to lose her teaching position. During this time she discerned religious life and entered a Carmelite convent in 1934. She took the name Sr. Teresa Benedicta of the Cross.

There was a rising occurrence of Jewish persecution, so Sr. Teresa was brought to Holland for safety. There she stayed until July of 1942, when she was arrested and taken to a concentration camp. She was killed in the gas chamber at Auschwitz on August 9, 1942. Through it all, Sr. Teresa Benedicta of the Cross maintained a tremendous sense of peace in the midst of persecution and death.

The words of St. Teresa Benedicta of the Cross

" For by doing what God demands of us with total surrender of our innermost being, we cause the divine life to become our own inner life. Entering into ourselves, we find God in our own selves."

In 1998, St. Teresa Benedicta of the Cross—the Jewish girl who converted to Catholicism, entered a convent and was killed in the Jewish Holocaust—was canonized by St. John Paul II.

The Fruit of Peace

"Peace Train"..."Give Peace a Chance"..."We Want Peace"... The list of songs that are inspired by peace go on and on. What is peace? Is it merely the absence of war or conflict? One merely needs to pick up a newspaper or watch the evening news to realize that there isn't peace in our world. But many times there isn't peace in our country, our communities, or our families. Because it is not only war that causes peace to be nonexistent. It is also such issues as gang violence, alcohol and other drug abuse, physical and sexual abuse, depression and suicide, and countless other ways that keep us from peace.

The word *peace* comes from the Latin word *pax*. *Peace* in Hebrew is *shalom*. *Shalom* (a word that Jesus would have used many times!) means a certain wholeness or completeness in one's relationship. When a Jewish person wants to wish another peace or tranquility, he or she says, "*Shalom.*" It is used as both a greeting and a sending forth.

Jesus, the "Prince of Peace," wants the relationships that exist between all peoples, regardless of background, religion, or gender (and so much more!) to be grounded in *shalom*—to be grounded in peace. In fact, in his famous Sermon on the Mount, the Beatitudes include: "Blessed are the peacemakers, for they will be called sons and daughters of God."

How can we give peace a chance in our lives? Here are four ways you might consider as you try to relate to those around you. These ways come from Stephen Covey's *7 Habits of Highly Effective People:*

1. **Be proactive.** Do not let disagreements fester into something bigger. Face the situations head on and do it early enough so that the conflict doesn't get bigger.

2. **Begin with the end in mind:** What is it that you want your relationship to look like? You will not achieve that relationship unless you can picture it!

3. **Think win-win:** There don't have to be winners and losers in every aspect of our lives. What if we both win? What would that look like? Begin there!

4. **Seek first to understand—then to be understood:** We usually want people to understand us and our point

of view. Once that is achieved, all will be right with the world. Right? Wrong! First try to understand where the other person is coming from. Then help them to understand your point of view. Only then!

St. John XXIII wrote: "May Christ inflame the desires of all men [and women] to break through the barriers which divide them, to strengthen the bonds of mutual love, to learn to understand one another, and to pardon those who have done them wrong. Through His power and inspiration may all peoples welcome each other to their hearts as brothers [and sisters], and may the peace they long for ever flower and ever reign among them" (Encyclical letter, *Peace on Earth*, 171).

The words of St. Teresa Benedicta of the Cross

““ Love is stronger than hatred. In the end there will be only the fullness of love...If we accept the whole Christ in faithful self-giving, by choosing and walking in the way of the imitation of Christ, then he will lead us through his Passion and Cross to the glory of the Resurrection."

Reflect

In your everyday life can you name examples of the living peace of Christ? Are there examples where this peace is absent?

_____

_____

_____

_____

_____

_____

Act

Using the steps above how are you able to bring peace to an issue that you listed in the Reflection section?

_____

_____

_____

_____

_____

_____

CHAPTER ELEVEN

The Fruit of Patience

MODEL OF FAITH ▶ *St. Kateri Tekakwitha*

ST. KATERI TEKAKWITHA IS THE FIRST NATIVE AMERICAN PERSON TO BE CANONIZED. She endured a hard and difficult life. But through it all her wisdom shone through. Kateri was an Algonquin-Mohawk woman who was born in the Mohawk village of Ossernenon, New York, in 1656. Her entire family was struck by smallpox when she was four years old. The rest of her family died from the disease. While Kateri lived, her face was scarred very badly—so much so that she covered it with a blanket on most occasions for the remainder of her life. She was adopted by her father's sister and her husband and raised by them.

At the age of nineteen, Kateri, influenced by the Jesuit priests who were evangelizing Native Americans, converted to Catholicism. She was given the name Catherine, after Catherine of Siena. In the native language this became Kateri.

While it would have been customary for her to marry and have children, she refused to do so. Instead, she left her village and moved to Kahnawake, which is just south of Montreal, Quebec, Canada. There she remained single and a virgin until her death at the age of 24. Her later life had been one of great hardship as she was shunned by her tribe for her refusal to marry.

Kateri Tekakwitha is known as the Lily of the Mohawks. She was canonized by Pope Benedict XVI in October 2012.

The Fruit of Patience

Patience actually has two different meanings and both are important for our understanding of, and living, the fruit of patience. On the one hand, patience can mean holding one's temper in check. The opposite, of course, would be losing our temper and taking revenge on the one who has wronged us. It takes great patience (think of a little brother or sister's annoying behavior!) to resist an outburst, to refrain from losing our temper.

On the other hand, patience can also mean endurance. Let's face it, when life presents us with some struggles— such as a loss of a job, a teacher who piles on the homework, a breakup in a relationship— we can lack patience. But life is worth living for the long haul. Like an athlete who keeps fighting for victory, even in the face of sure defeat, a person with patience sees the long view and lives with that end in mind.

The words of St. Kateri Tekakwitha

"Who will teach me what is most pleasing to God, that I may do it?"

So how do you become a more patient person? While it is not easy, it *is* possible. Try these steps toward patience:

1. **Breathe deeply!** Filling your lungs and body with oxygen helps you to think more clearly, settle

yourself, and relax. If you feel yourself in an uncomfortable or stressful situation, then stop. Take a few deep cleansing breaths, and then let yourself find a good, deep rhythm of breathing. It will make a world of difference!

2   **Consider what makes you impatient.** What is the root cause? If you can name what makes you impatient it will go a long way toward dealing with this feeling. Is it something your parent says? How about a teacher? Or a sibling? If you can name it, you can claim more control over your impatience.

3   **Use active listening skills to really listen to what other people are saying.** In our hurriedness sometimes we do not listen as we should. But if you can slow down and really listen attentively to another person, it will lead to greater understanding, which leads to patience.

4   Along these same lines, **try to understand a situation from another person's point of view**. If we can "get out of our skin" a little and try to understand a situation from another person's point of view, we can usually have more patience with the person involved.

5   **Practicing delayed gratification can lead to greater patience.** If we can wait for something or someone, and not demand that something occur this very minute, we can develop a greater sense of patience.

6   Most importantly, **praying for patience can actually lead to greater patience**. Ask God for the courage and strength to be more patient. You might be amazed at how much more patient you will become!

St. Paul, while he was in prison and writing to the people of Ephesus, said it quite well: "I, then, a prisoner for the Lord, urge you to live in a manner worthy of the call you have received, with all humility and gentleness, with patience, bearing with one another through love" (Ephesians 4:1–2).

God has been patient with us! Now God calls us to be patient with ourselves and with each other! Parents or friends who sometimes annoy, hurt, confound, or dismiss us cause us to lack patience. As St. Paul reminds us, we are called to have great patience during these times. Come Holy Spirit! Help us to have patience!

The words of St. Kateri Tekakwitha

" I am not my own; I have given myself to Jesus. He must be my only love."

Reflect

Of the six steps towards patience listed above, what step do you thrive at?

_____

_____

_____

_____

What step do you find to be the greatest challenge?

_____

_____

_____

_____

_____

Act

For the next three days, be conscious of the times when your patience is tested. When you get into those situations, count to three before responding or reacting. Then, look at the situation you were in and reflect upon how you felt in your delayed response.

Example: Your parent tells you to take out the garbage while you are watching your favorite TV show.

CHAPTER TWELVE

The Fruit of Kindness

MODEL OF FAITH ▸ *St. Maximilian Kolbe*

IS THERE ANY GREATER KINDNESS THAN LAYING DOWN YOUR LIFE FOR ANOTHER PERSON? In the Gospel of John, Jesus states: "No one has greater love than this, to lay down one's life for one's friends" (John 15:13). That is exactly what St. Maximilian Kolbe did in the midst of World War II.

Maximilian Kolbe was born in Poland in 1894. After struggling with health issues throughout his childhood, Maximilian entered the seminary and became a priest. Maximilian organized several religious groups or congregations including the Knights of Mary Immaculate, City of the Immaculate, and the Conventual Friars.

The Nazis invaded Poland in 1939. Because he hid a number of Jewish people from the Nazi regime, Maximilian was arrested, with other priests and religious, in February 1941 and sent to the Auschwitz concentration camp. When three prisoners escaped, the camp commander gave orders for ten other prisoners to be starved to death to keep others from thinking of escaping too. One of the men chosen was Francis Gajowniczek, a married man with young children. Maximilian stepped in and offered to take the man's place.

While in the death chamber Maximilian led the other

men in prayer and reflection. After a month Maximilian was the only one of the ten still alive. So the Nazis injected him with a lethal serum.

Saint John Paul II, like Maximilian, was from Poland. In 1982, the Holy Father canonized Maximilian Kolbe. Francis Gajowniczek, the man whose life was spared as Maximilian gave his, was present for the celebration.

The Fruit of Kindness

How many times have you done something in the hopes that something would be coming your way in return? You clean your bedroom so that you can use the car to go out with friends. You mow the lawn so that you can go to a friend's lake home for the weekend. You do your homework without being told so that...

Wait a minute! Shouldn't you do your homework without being told? Seriously, all of these examples are not what the Scripture writers had in mind when they described God as kind and loving.

What is kindness? Kindness is that trait of ours that does good

> ❝ **The words of St. Maximilian Kolbe**
>
> Let us remember that love lives through sacrifice and is nourished by giving...Without sacrifice there is no love."

with nothing expected in return. You have no doubt heard of a random act of kindness or the concept of "paying it forward." In both cases, a person does something nice for another without any expectation of a reward. A person is at a tollbooth and pays the toll for the next car. A person fixes a flat tire for a stranded driver on the freeway. Instead of accepting payment for the good deed, the person instead asks the driver to do something kind for someone else in the future.

What would the world be like if we looked for ways to be kind to one another? Perhaps you have heard the song "The Christmas Shoes." The story is about a boy who wants to purchase a pair of shoes for his dying mother. Unfortunately, when he gets to the cash register and lays down his money the boy realizes he doesn't have enough to pay for the shoes. Seeing this all take place, the writer of the song, who happens to be in line behind the boy, offers to pay for the shoes. The boy, the mother, and the kind man who donated the money will truly have a merrier Christmas. Why? Because of a kind act of a man who expected nothing in return.

We are not all called to be Maximilian Kolbes. We will not all give our lives as martyrs. But we can all be on the lookout to do kind acts and be kind people. It begins with one kind act at a time!

Reflect

What does it feel like to perform a random act of kindness?

_____

_____

_____

_____

What does it feel like to be on the receiving end of a random act of kindness?

_____

_____

_____

_____

Act

Consider performing a random act of kindness. Some examples might include:

- Sit next to the young person in the lunchroom who is eating alone.

- Pay for the customer in line behind you at the local fast food restaurant.

- Mow the lawn of a neighbor without being told.

CHAPTER THIRTEEN

The Fruit of Goodness

MODEL OF FAITH

Catherine de Hueck Doherty

CATHERINE DE HUECK DOHERTY WAS BORN IN RUSSIA IN 1896. She was raised Catholic by a Polish Catholic father. When she was fifteen, Catherine married a baron, Boris de Hueck. Early in their marriage, World War I broke out and both were involved in battle—Boris as an officer in the army and Catherine as a nurse. Each certainly saw the horror of war.

Following the war, the de Huecks were on the run for several years because they were part of the aristocracy that had been overthrown during the Russian Revolution. They first went to Finland and finally ended up in Canada. At one point, Catherine took on a job as a sales clerk in a department store in New York City. There she was approached by a woman who asked Catherine to enter into the speaking circuit to tell her story. Catherine did so and accumulated wealth that afforded her many luxuries. But she was driven to help the poor. So she moved into an apartment in the slums of Toronto that she called Friendship House. She wanted to live "the gospel without compromise."

Dorothy Day, co-founder of the Catholic Worker Movement, was instrumental in Catherine's ministry. Both shared the same vision and passion in their work with the poor. Catherine opened up a second Friendship House in New York City's Harlem area. Thomas Merton was another contemporary of Catherine's and was inspired by her work.

After Boris de Hueck died, Catherine married Eddie Doherty, thus becoming Catherine de Hueck Doherty. She opened a new community that she called Madonna House, which became a house of prayer and a place for retreat. Catherine died in 1985.

The Fruit of Goodness

In Psalm 23:6, the famous "Good Shepherd" psalm, the psalmist writes that "surely goodness and kindness will follow me all of the days of my life." Goodness and kindness are two sides of one coin. One follows the other and vice versa.

Earlier in the psalm, the writer points out that God is walking with him, helping him to relax, setting a table for him, anointing him, and comforting him. That is a lot of goodness and kindness! But what is the ultimate sign that these fruits will be a part of his life? The psalmist states that he will dwell with God in God's house forever. In other words, the writer is making a promise that he will stick with God through thick and thin, through good times and in bad. And God will do the same. And for that reason, the writer is confident that the ultimate goodness, dwelling in God's love for eternity, will be his reward.

Just like the Psalmist, we have been blessed with so much goodness in our life. And the Holy Spirit promises to provide us with the fruit of even more goodness in the days ahead.

Like Catherine de Hueck Doherty, we might be faced with some difficult challenges and obstacles. But our faith in Jesus challenges us to reach out to others whose challenges most likely are even greater than ours and to be of service to these "least of our brothers and sisters." Catherine gives us a great model of counting our blessings, dealing with our challenges, and blessing the lives of others with our love and service. For goodness sake, let's get started!

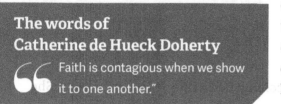

The words of Catherine de Hueck Doherty

" Faith is contagious when we show it to one another."

Reflect

How aware are you of the goodness in your life?

_____

_____

_____

_____

_____

_____

Do you look at only the negative and darkness in your life?
Or can you truly count your blessings—the goodness—in
your life? How so?

_____

_____

_____

_____

_____

_____

_____

_____

_____

_____

_____

Act

Choose an action this week that will be of service to another
person. Send a card, note, or letter with words of gratitude,
pointing out where you have seen the goodness in those who
were able to serve.

CHAPTER FOURTEEN

The Fruit of Generosity

MODEL OF FAITH — *Dorothy Day*

CAN THERE BE ANYTHING MORE GENEROUS THAN OPENING UP A HOUSE OF HOSPITALITY AND DEDICATING YOUR LIFE TO THE POOR? That is exactly what Dorothy Day did! Dorothy Day was born in Brooklyn, New York, in 1897. Though baptized as an Episcopalian, she had very little religious upbringing. By the time she entered college she had virtually no religious life at all. She became a journalist and worked for some communist publications in her early adult years.

In 1926 she became pregnant and gave birth to a daughter. She had a deep sense of the love of God and felt it necessary to have the child baptized as a Catholic. This caused great distress in her life, because the man she lived with, and who fathered her daughter, did not believe in either religion or marriage. A separation was inevitable.

In 1932 Dorothy met Peter Maurin, a French philosopher who had strong beliefs about poverty and the Works of Mercy. Together they started the Catholic Worker newspaper. The newspaper afforded them the opportunity to open a House of Hospitality on the Lower East Side of New York for those who were struggling in the midst of the Great Depression.

Dorothy Day became an antiwar protester from World War II to the Vietnam War. She was jailed many times for her actions for peace. She maintained an incredible balance between personal and public prayer, along with her service work and works of justice. Dorothy died on November 29, 1980.

In the fall of 2015, when Pope Francis addressed the United States Congress, he used these words as he spoke about Dorothy: "In these times when social concerns are so important, I cannot fail to mention the Servant of God Dorothy Day, who founded the Catholic Worker Movement. Her social activism, her passion for justice and the cause of the oppressed, were inspired by the Gospel, her faith, and the example of the saints." On April 19, 2016, Cardinal Timothy Dolan of New York opened up her cause for canonization. Hopefully, one day we will be calling her St. Dorothy for her kind and generous spirit!

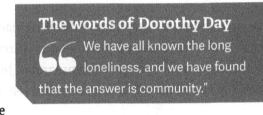

The words of Dorothy Day

We have all known the long loneliness, and we have found that the answer is community."

The Fruit of Generosity

The fruit of generosity can easily be linked with stewardship. In the Scriptures, a steward was someone who took care of another person's property. The property was not owned by the steward. The steward merely took care of the property. Do you consider yourself a steward in today's world?

The classic way to look at stewardship today is through the three words: time, talent, treasure. Another, yet similar, way to view stewardship is through three other words: prayer, service, and sharing. How much do you generously give in these three areas? Disciples of Jesus, those who are committed to following Jesus, need to examine these areas.

Prayer: Once you see your life as devoted to God, without separation between prayer and other aspects of your life, you will begin to fully realize the depth and dimensions of discipleship!

Service: Taking time on a regular basis to reach out in generous service to the poor and marginalized, in all of its various ways, is following the command of Jesus to serve him in serving the "least of our brothers and sisters."

Sharing: The next time that you go to the mall and purchase an article of clothing, look into your closet and determine what you can give away to the local clothes closet or thrift shop.

When our lives are centered around these three aspects of stewardship and generosity—prayer, service, and sharing— then our lives will be centered on the generosity that Jesus calls us to. That is what Dorothy Day did every day of her life. May we do the same!

The words of Dorothy Day

" Don't call me a saint. I don't want to be dismissed so easily."

Reflect

Prayer—How aware are you of God's presence in your life? How do you communicate this with God?

_____

_____

_____

_____

Service—Who are the persons in your life whom you could serve? How can you serve these persons in need?

_____

_____

_____

Sharing—How generous are you in sharing the resources that you have?

_____

_____

_____

_____

Act

PRAYER

Choose a time and space in your life where you can listen to God by:

- Reading the Bible

- Listening to Christian music

- Reading an inspirational story of a saint

- Attending an extra Mass on a weekday

SERVICE

Choose a time and place to serve others in need by:

- Serving a meal at a local homeless shelter

- Visiting an elderly person in a nursing home

- Being a listening friend to someone who is having a difficult time in life

- Performing an extra chore around the house

SHARING

Choose a manner in which you can share more of your resources by:

- Putting money in the church collection basket

- Organizing a collection for a local charitable cause

- Becoming a mentor or tutor in your school

CHAPTER FIFTEEN

The Fruit of Gentleness

MODEL OF FAITH — *Thomas Merton*

THOMAS MERTON IS CONSIDERED ONE OF THE GREATEST CONTEMPLATIVES OF THE TWENTIETH CENTURY. With that came his incredible gentleness as a person and Trappist monk.

Thomas was born in Prades, France, in 1915. His mother died early in his childhood and Thomas lived a rather wild life. He eventually made his way to the United States. It was while attending Columbia University that Thomas converted to Catholicism. He entered Gethsemani Abbey, a Trappist monastery near Louisville, Kentucky, three days after the bombing of Pearl Harbor and the United States entry into World War II in 1941.

Thomas spent twenty-seven years at Gethsemani and became a prolific author. He wrote over sixty books and numerous articles on spirituality, contemplation, and prayer. His most famous work is his autobiography, *The Seven Storey Mountain*, published in 1948. It became an instant bestseller and gave a glimpse into the life of a monastery as well as into the life of a young man who had traveled a journey to the monastic life.

He also became an outspoken voice in the Civil Rights Movement as well as the Vietnam War. It was this balance—

between engagement in the world and encounter with the spiritual life—that made Thomas Merton so popular. One of his most profound moments came on March 18, 1958, in Louisville. He was standing on the corner of Fourth Street and Walnut when a profound sensation struck him—one that he later wrote about: "I was suddenly overwhelmed with the realization that I loved all those people, that they were mine and I theirs, that we could not be alien to one another even though we were total strangers. It was like waking from a dream of separateness, of spurious self-isolation in a special world, the world of renunciation and supposed holiness."

The words of Thomas Merton

" Love is our true destiny. We do not find the meaning of life by ourselves alone—we find it with another."

Thomas went on to become interested in Eastern religions, and he played a pivotal role in discussions between Catholicism and some Eastern spiritualities. It was in 1968, shortly after delivering a presentation in Bangkok (his first visit out of the country since becoming a monk) that he was accidentally electrocuted by touching an electric fan while stepping onto a wet bathroom floor after a shower. This gentle spirit who had touched so many lives, and continues to do so through his writing, was sent home to God.

The Fruit of Gentleness

Jesus was truly countercultural! In a time when "an eye for an eye, and a tooth for a tooth" ruled the day, Jesus brought a different message—be gentle with one another. Love one another. Gentleness is that fruit of the Holy Spirit that calls us to be tender and mild mannered with everyone and everything we meet.

In the Beatitudes, Jesus used the phrase "Blessed are the meek." What did Jesus mean by this? He was calling on his followers to be humble and kind to each other. He was calling his followers to resist judging or harming others. How different that must have sounded to a people who lived in a land that consistently experienced war, violence, and discontent. It still does today!

But it is a countercultural message for us in the twenty-first century as well. Gentleness is not always our strongest suit. In fact, when you scan the movie listings at your local theater, or check the TV options for a show tonight, you will find plenty of dramas and thrillers that include lots of violence. On average, children watch four hours of TV per day. By the time they are eighteen they will have witnessed 200,000 acts of violence and 16,000 murders on TV. Researchers have found that children who watch this much violence on TV tend to be less sensitive to the suffering of others and more fearful of the world around them, and may act out more violently in their relationships with others.

Some of the greatest peace advocates in history had a sense of being gentle while making their position heard

> ### The words of Thomas Merton
>
> " Love seeks one thing only: the good of the one loved. It leaves all the other secondary effects to take care of themselves. Love, therefore, is its own reward."

and felt. Jesus, Gandhi, Martin Luther King Jr., and Thomas Merton, our model of faith for this chapter, all were gentle people (gentlemen, as it were!) But each of them took stands for something or against something and did it in a non-violent, peaceful way.

One way to examine your own life in terms of gentleness is to take a hard look at how we view media. We need to assess our media literacy. Here are three ways that you can be a more literate media consumer, whether listening to music, watching TV or a movie, or even viewing billboards on the freeway:

1   *Audiences and authors:* It is important to know that authors of media—any media—know who you are as a consumer. And there is a reason they want you viewing their media. Generally this is either to make money or gain political power. Knowing that media is produced for a reason is the first step in becoming media literate.

2   *Meanings and messages:* All media come with a message. As an active consumer of media you can participate in trying to figure out what messages are contained in any medium you consume. Do you really listen to the words of a song? What are the messages in the words? Media consumption is a participation activity—not a passive action.

3   *Representations and reality:* All media are produced using certain techniques. And the techniques are used to get a certain message across to the audience. And the producer of the media influences what that message is. As an active and literate media consumer, you can try to figure out what techniques are used and what values the producer of the media is promoting. In a car ad, for example, what does the inclusion of a beautiful young woman tell us about the performance of the automobile? Why is she included in the ad?

In a violent and troubled world, Jesus calls us, by the power of the Holy Spirit, to create a new reality—one shaped by love and peace. Gentleness is a place to begin. And media literacy is one way to create this Reign of God in a concrete way. You can get started right now—by using media literacy the next time you watch a show or listen to a song!

Reflect

Reflect on a song or an ad:

How does this song or ad make you feel?

_____

_____

_____

_____

_____

_____

_____

What message does the song or ad provide?

_____

_____

_____

_____

How does this message measure up to the love and gentle
compassion that Jesus calls us to have toward ourselves and
others?

_____

_____

_____

_____

_____

Act

Listen to the radio or watch TV for an hour. Use the three
media literacy techniques to become more literate and
engaged in what you are watching and listening to.

CHAPTER SIXTEEN

The Fruit of Faithfulness

MODEL OF FAITH — *St. Peter Claver*

ST. PETER CLAVER WAS A MODEL OF FAITHFULNESS TO THE MOST POOR AND VULNERABLE. Born in 1581, Claver became a Jesuit priest. He was sent to serve the people of Cartagena, Colombia, in 1610. Cartagena was a busy port serving as an entry point for African slaves to the New World. Ten thousand slaves arrived every year in Cartagena to work in the mines of the Americas.

While the work in the mines was very hard and dangerous, the passage from Africa to the Americas also killed many slaves, sometimes up to a third of them. Stowed away in cargo holds, given very little food or drink, and struck with illness, the slaves often died en route. Once they arrived in Cartagena, the slaves needed much care. This is where St. Peter comes into the picture.

Once a slave ship arrived in port, Peter Claver would meet the ship and minister to the half-dead men and women aboard. He treated their wounds, gave them food and drink, and with the help of interpreters, communicated the message of Christianity to them. Think how the slaves must have first received him! Christianity was the religion of the slave owners. But the difference with Peter's message is that he shared with them God's unconditional love for them.

Their faith was to be grounded in human dignity. This was a different message for a starving, sick, and hurting people.

Over a forty-year period, Peter Claver ministered to thousands of slaves, baptizing over 300,000 of them. He even carried his ministry to the fields and mines, becoming a person who cared for them spiritually and physically.

Peter was struck with the plague in 1650. Physically, he was never the same again. He died a lonely, sick man on September 8, 1654. He was canonized in 1888, and in the United States his feast day is September 9.

The Fruit of Faithfulness

Sometimes the meaning of a fruit of the Holy Spirit is provided simply in the word of the fruit. In this case, *faithfulness* is defined by someone who is full of faith in any situation. There are so many examples of faithfulness in all walks of life. For example:

The married couple who remains married for seventy years, despite years of hardship including the death of children, job loss, and personal health challenges. Each of them could have called it quits many times. Yet they remained faithful day after day, year after year.

A person who remains faithful to a friendship even when it is rejected for a time—for example, when his or her friend spends all of their time with a boyfriend or girlfriend, or with another friendship group. The person could have gone his or her separate way but instead remained faithful to the relationship.

The young man who accepted a scholarship to a Division 1 university in basketball. But his talents have the National Basketball Association calling, with a promise that he will be selected in the upcoming draft. He remembers the confidence that his college coach showed in him as he offered the scholarship and developed him as a player. So, he shows faithfulness to his coach and school and declines the overtures of the NBA by coming back to college and his team for his senior year.

So how do you become a more faithful person? Jesus gave the secret two thousand years ago. In Luke 16:10–11 Jesus says: "The person who is trustworthy in very small matters is also trustworthy in great ones; and the person who is dishonest in very small matters is also dishonest in great ones. If, therefore, you are not trustworthy with dishonest wealth, who will trust you with true wealth?" So the development of faithfulness is a long-haul operation. There are no shortcuts. There are no easy paths. Keep the faith!

Reflect

As a person who is striving to be a faithful follower of Jesus, how are you doing in your relationships with self, others, and God?

How do you continue to grow in understanding yourself?

_____

_____

_____

What steps are you taking to build relationships with others?

_____

_____

_____

How does a positive relationship with yourself and others help you to grow spiritually closer to God?

_____

_____

_____

If you are faithful in these little things, truly you will remain faithful in bigger elements of your life as well. How can you know? Jesus told us so! Are you full of faith? Are you faithful?

Act

Choose an act that challenges you to be faithful. Find the strength and courage within yourself to have faith in what you desire to accomplish. Then JUST DO IT!!!

CHAPTER SEVENTEEN

The Fruit of Modesty

 MODEL OF FAITH *St. Thérèse of Lisieux*

THÉRÈSE WAS BORN IN 1873 IN LISIEUX, NORMANDY, FRANCE. Therese's mother died when she was four. Her two older sisters entered a Carmelite convent in their late teens, and Thérèse begged her father to let her do the same. At the young age of fifteen, she received permission to do so.

Thérèse's life was short. She died at the age of 24 of tuberculosis. But she made the most of her years. She wrote an autobiography, entitled *The Story of a Soul*. In it she described her own spiritual life. Two aspects of her life became an instant model for others.

First, she described her method of spirituality, which she termed "the Little Way." Simply put, the Little Way was seeing each moment of one's life, both those events when we celebrate and those moments when we suffer, as filled with the presence and love of God. Each moment of life presented an opportunity to transform the world.

Second, Thérèse believed that she was suited to many different vocations—many walks of life. From a warrior, to a martyr, to a priest, she felt called to many different ways of living.

Thérèse called herself "The Little Flower." She felt that,

while she was precious in the eyes of God, she was of little account or importance. Millions around the world know her by this title.

Thérèse contracted tuberculosis and suffered great pain from the disease. She died in 1897. Many miracles were ascribed to Thérèse in the years following her death. Her canonization process was incredibly fast. She was declared a saint in 1925, only twenty-eight years after her death. Her feast day is October 1, and she was named a doctor of the church—one of the great teachers of our faith.

> ## The words of St. Thérèse of Lisieux
>
> " I applied myself above all to practice quite hidden little acts of virtue; thus I liked to fold the mantles forgotten by the Sisters, and sought a thousand opportunities of rendering them service."

The Fruit of Modesty

The *Catechism of the Catholic Church* instructs us that "teaching modesty to children and adolescents means awakening in them respect for the human person" (CCC, #2524). When we respect each person as a unique creation of God, we are truly acting in a modest way, inspired by the fruit of modesty.

The word *modesty* has two meanings. First, it includes how we dress and look. But it also means how we carry ourselves as a person. You have undoubtedly heard the expression: "Oh, she is just being modest." When said this way, it almost seems as though the person is trying to hide the person whom God created. And sometimes this is a false modesty that is equally a misrepresentation of one's true self. The extreme opposites of modesty are boldness, pride, and conceit. Which person do you want to be?

St. Thérèse of Lisieux, the Little Flower, provides an inspirational example of modesty. She was modest without confusing this for some false modesty. She saw herself as a beautiful flower, created in the image and likeness of God. But she did this in such an honest, mature, and humble fashion. Come, Holy Spirit, and help us to be modest as Jesus and St. Thérèse of Lisieux were modest!

Reflect

When you look into the mirror what do you see? How do you see beauty and goodness? What messages from others, both positive and negative, are being reflected there?

_____

_____

_____

_____

Act

Think of the person whom you admire most. List all of the admirable characteristics of that person. Put a star next to the characteristics that you feel that you possess as well. Put an X next to those characteristics that you would like to work on more.

[CHAPTER EIGHTEEN]

The Fruit
of Self-Control

MODEL
OF FAITH

Joseph Cardinal Bernardin

BORN IN 1928, JOSEPH BERNARDIN WAS
NAMED A BISHOP AT THE YOUNG AGE OF 38
IN 1966. There are a number of important
developments or events in Bernardin's life
for which he will forever be remembered.

In the early 1980s Bernardin was the president of the
National Conference of Catholic Bishops (now the United
States Conference of Catholic Bishops). He shepherded a
unique listening and writing process, through which the
conference produced "The Challenge of Peace," the famous
pastoral letter on peace in which the U.S. bishops voiced
their concern about war and the increasingly dangerous
arms build-up in nations around the world.

In the 1982, Bishop Bernardin became Archbishop of
Chicago and was later named a cardinal. During this time,
Bernardin developed the seamless garment, or consistent
ethic of life, approach that confronted a great division in the
church around issues of social justice, including abortion.
He followed this up by developing the Catholic Common
Ground Project in which he attempted to bring together the
two extreme poles in the church—conservative and liberal.

Cardinal Bernardin had to show great self-control when a young man brought a claim of misconduct against Bernardin. The man later withdrew his charges and Bernardin was cleared of any wrongdoing. But what made the episode particularly memorable is that Bernardin met with the young man and completely forgave him despite his false allegations.

Lastly, Bernardin contracted cancer. He courageously

> ## The words of
> ## Cardinal Joseph Bernardin
>
> " What I would like to leave behind is a simple prayer that each of you may find what I have found—God's special gift to us all: the gift of peace. When we are at peace, we find the freedom to be most fully who we are, even in the worst of times. We let go of what is nonessential and embrace what is essential. We empty ourselves so that God may more fully work within us. And we become instruments in the hands of the Lord."

showed the church and the world how to gracefully and peacefully live while dying. Cardinal Bernardin died of pancreatic cancer on November 14, 1996, at the age of 68.

The Fruit of Self-Control

The fruit of self-control helps us to balance our needs and desires so that we do not go overboard in either category. One of the areas needed for self-control is in our purchasing habits. Just turn on the TV for fifteen minutes and you are sure to see at least six commercials providing you with the same message—you NEED this product!

But you can also exercise self-control by living a balanced life in other areas as well. When we get enough sleep, and eat proper foods, we are living a life of self-control. When we get a proper amount of exercise or limit the number of hours we watch TV or use social media such as Twitter or Snapchat, we are also using self-control.

The Holy Spirit comes to us with an inspirational message: in all things use moderation. The ultimate issue is determining the difference between "wants" and "needs." A "want" is something that we desire but is not essential for living. A "need" is something we must have in order to make it in life. When we have a proper perspective on wants and needs, we can truly live with self-control.

There is an ultimate freedom in this self-control. When we are controlled by something or someone, we are imprisoned by that control. When we use self-control in our relationships, our spending, and our use of time, we have the greatest freedom available to us as humans. As Jesus said, "the truth shall set you free!" With the fruit of self-control, the Holy Spirit shows us this path to freedom.

Reflect

What do you really value or desire in life? List the ten things that give you the most pleasure in life:

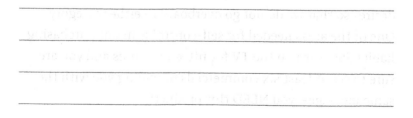

Now go back and check those items that you absolutely could not live without. What are those items? Are they people? Are they possessions?

Act

Over the next week take note of how much time you spend on social media. Note the hours spent each day below:

Sunday _____

Monday _____

Tuesday _____

Wednesday _____

Thursday _____

Friday _____

Saturday _____

How much freedom do you have in your use of social media?

[CHAPTER NINETEEN]
The Fruit of Chastity

MODEL OF FAITH

Mary, the Mother of God

MARY, OR MIRIAM IN HEBREW, WAS A TEENAGER WHEN GOD SENT THE ANGEL GABRIEL TO A SMALL TOWN IN GALILEE NAMED NAZARETH. The angel encountered Mary at her house and invited her to become the mother of Jesus, who would become the savior of the world. There was only one problem with this in the eyes of the young Mary. She was not yet married to Joseph and she had been chaste all of her life. She remained a virgin—pure both in her heart and with her body. The angel instructed Mary that she would conceive by the power of the Holy Spirit and would give birth to Jesus. Mary replied that all of this should be done according to God's will.

Mary, a virgin, gave birth to Jesus. And she remained pure in body, mind, and spirit her entire life. Because of this she was later assumed into heaven, both body and soul.

We celebrate Mary on many different feasts in the church year. For example,

Mary, the Holy Mother of God (January 1)
The Annunciation of the Lord (March 25)
The Visitation of the Blessed Virgin Mary (May 31)
The Assumption of the Blessed Virgin Mary (August 15)

The Nativity of the Blessed Virgin Mary (September 8)

The Immaculate Conception (December 8)

There are numerous other special days when we honor Mary. She is a model of faith, especially in her purity and chastity.

The Fruit of Chastity

Chastity comes from a Latin word meaning "pure." We can remain pure in many ways. At its core, the purity that guides all of our actions and thoughts is purity of heart. When we have a pure heart, filled with love for all people and all things—including the earth—then our actions will follow. When we act purely, or chastely, then our mind and heart will be affected and we will think and feel with purity as well. A term for this is the Greek word *orthopraxy*. It means "right living." When we live right—live pure—our minds and hearts will follow along. Our relationships with others will be affected too as we treat them as persons created in the image and likeness of God.

Jesus said to his followers, "Truly I tell you, unless you change and become like little children, you will never enter the kingdom of heaven" (Matthew 18:3). Being pure of heart is living life through the innocence of a child.

Mary, the Mother of God, is an amazing example of this fruit of chastity or purity. Her ability to live *orthopraxy*, to live rightly, gives us an example to follow. And like her, we can honestly state that "All things are possible with God."

Reflect

On a scale of 1 to 10 how would you rate your ability to see life through the eyes of a child?

_____

_____

_____

What gets in the way of living life with a pure heart?

_____

_____

_____

What unique characteristics of Mary's life do you admire?

_____

_____

_____

Act

Create an artistic expression that brings a childlike sense of wonder and joy to your life. Examples might include:

- Writing a poem
- Drawing a picture
- Painting a portrait
- Playing a musical instrument